MW00880024

Port & the Douro

Intelligent Guides to Wines & Top Vineyards

Benjamin Lewin MW

Copyright © 2016 Benjamin Lewin

Vendange Press

Ver 1.03 06-16

ISBN-13: 978-153542998

www.vendangepress.com

This Guide is devoted specifically to Port and the Douro. The first part discusses the region and its wines, explaining the character and range of the wines, including the various types of Port and the table wines, both red and white, that are being increasingly made in the Douro. The second part has individual profiles of the top producers, showing how each winemaker interprets that character.

In the first part I address the nature of the wines made today and ask how this has changed, how it's driven by tradition or competition, and how styles may evolve in the future. I show how the wines are related to the terroir and to the types of grape varieties that are grown, and I explain the classification system.

There's no single definition for what constitutes a top producer. Leading producers range from those who are so prominent as to represent the common public face of an appellation to those who demonstrate an unexpected potential on a tiny scale. The producers profiled in the guide should represent the best of both tradition and innovation in wine in the region

In the individual profiles, I have tried to give a sense of each producer's aims for his wines, of the personality and philosophy behind them—to meet the person who makes the wine, as it were, as much as to review the wines themselves. For each producer I suggest reference wines that are a good starting point for understanding his style. Most of the producers welcome visits, although some require appointments: details are in the profiles.

The guide is based on many visits to producers over recent years. I owe an enormous debt to those who cooperated in this venture by engaging in discussion and opening innumerable bottles for tasting. This guide would not have been possible without them.

How to read the producer profiles

The second part of this guide consists of profiles of individual wine producers. Each profile shows a sample label, a picture of the winery, and details of production, followed by a description of the producer and winemaker. The producer's rating (from one to three stars) is shown to the right of the name.

The profiles are organized geographically, and each group of profiles is preceded by a map showing the locations of starred producers to help plan itineraries.

A full list of the symbols used in the profiles appears at the start of the profile section. This is an example of a profile:

Hotel Dieu, Beaune, France
address

03 80 24 44 02

Catherine Guillemot

catherine.guillemot@ch-beaune.fr

Vintage Port fortified reference wine

Beaune 1er, Nicolas Rolin
red reference wine

Corton Charlemagne, Charlotte Dumay
white reference wine

www.hospices-de-beaune.com

details of producer
60 ha; 400,000 bottles
vineyards & production

The Hospices de Beaune was founded in 1443 by Nicolas Rolin, chancellor of Burgundy, as a hospital for the poor. Standing in the heart of Beaune, the original buildings of the Hotel Dieu, now converted into a museum, surround a courtyard where an annual auction of wines was first held in 1859. The wines come from vineyards held as part of the endowment of the Hospices, and are sold in November to negociants who then take possession of the barrels and mature the wines in their own styles. (Today the auction is held in the modern covered marketplace opposite the Hotel Dieu.) There are 45 cuvées (32 red and 13 white); most come from premier or grand crus from the Côte de Beaune or Côte de Nuits, but because holdings are small (depending on past donations of land to the Hospices) many cuvées consist of blends from different crus (and are identified by brand names). The vines are cultivated, and the wine is made, by the Hospices. For some years the vineyards of the Hospices were not tended as carefully as they might have been, and the winemaking was less than perfect, but the appointment of a new régisseur has led to improvements in the present century. The name of the Hospices is only a starting point, because each negociant stamps his own style on the barriques he buys.

Contents

The Port Houses

Port owes its origins to English merchants who settled in Oporto after Portugal freed itself from Spanish rule and then in 1654 signed a trade treaty with England. They were essentially negociants who purchased grapes, made wine, and then shipped it abroad (mostly to England). Established along waterfront on the other side of the river in Oporto's sister city of Vila Nova de Gaia, the Port Houses formed the commercial center of the industry. Shippers along the waterfront on Gaia are fond of showing high water marks for where the flood waters reached in the famous floods of the twentieth century. The Lodges along the waterfront are now used as visitor centers. Most of the shippers have storage facilities higher up the hill to avoid the problem. Now that dams have been built, the river does not flood any more.

By the 1680s, the shippers were exporting fortified wine from the

Viewed from Oporto, Port Lodges line the river bank in Vila Nova Gaia to the right of the bridge.

Built in 1790 as the headquarters of the English merchants, the Factory House is a testament to their historic importance.

region around Régua to Britain. Fortification appears to have been introduced to preserve the wine and perhaps to give it more body. The wine was mostly fermented to dryness before adding brandy. Its style was lighter than the wines of today, but early in the eighteenth century, it was realized that adding brandy before the end of fermentation made the wine sweeter and stronger by retaining some sugar. It also became obvious that some time was required for the harshness to soften, and merchants began to age the wine in cask before exporting it. By the mid nineteenth century, Port was commonly sweet, with a level of alcohol similar to today, although from time to time there was criticism that the wine was being spoiled by the addition of brandy. At the end of the nineteenth century, virtually all Port was shipped in a traditional container called a Pipe (a large cask, about 550 liters) to Britain, where merchants would bottle it.

Port continued to be exported in cask until relatively recently. Bottling in London was more common than bottling in Portugal after the second world war. In 1970, it became mandatory to bottle

Barco rebelo sailing boats along the Douro were the only way of transporting wine from the vineyards to Oporto until relatively recently.

Vintage Port at source, and since 1997 all Port has been bottled locally.

Until 1987 it was a legal requirement that Port should be matured in Gaia, but today Port can be matured either in the Douro or in Gaia. It is much drier in the Douro, and there are seasonal changes of up to 20 C. (They used to talk about "Douro bake" for wines matured at source.) A cooler climate made Gaia a more suitable locale for maturing the Port, and most higher quality wines were matured there. Until the advent of air conditioning, the location made a significant difference, but today it makes less difference.

The Douro River

Less hospitable terrain for producing wine would be hard to imagine. Port is produced only in the Douro valley, which lies along the Douro river inland from the town of Oporto that gave its name to the wine. The mountainous terrain rises up sharply from the Douro river and its tributaries.

Vineyards rise up in very steep terraces from the Douro river.

Difficult to navigate, the Douro river was for long the sole source of transport through the region. Viticulture at first was possible only in the more western half, which today is divided into the lower (Baixo) and upper (Cima) Corgo. The Cachão de Valeira canyon, a huge granite outcrop, prevented navigation farther up the river. When this was removed in the mid eighteenth century, viticulture spread along the river to the Douro Superior in the east, extending to the Spanish border.

Vineyards run along the Douro river; the land is so steep and uninviting that often the area had to be dynamited to create the vineyards. (This is still true. When a vineyard was being planting recently at Quinta da Roriz, a huge boulder released by dynamite decapitated a pylon and cut off electricity to the local town.) Soils are stony, typically schist with very little subsoil. The bedrock is a hard granite. The terroir has often been altered greatly from its original

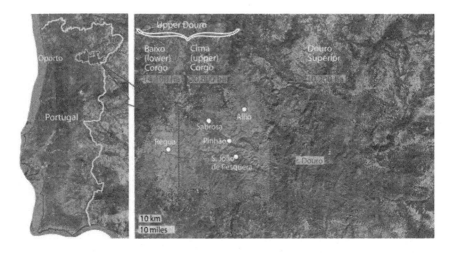

The Douro is divided into three regions

state by the extensive construction of terraces, rather narrow, and separated by stone walls. Ninety percent of the vineyards have slopes over 30 per cent, with some up to 70 per cent. Most grapes are grown at the lower elevations, although there are vineyards as high as 600 m. The best grapes are considered to come from close to the river (the local saying is that the best Port comes from grapes that can hear the river flowing).

Climate is different in each of the three regions. The mountains form a protective barrier against weather coming from the Atlantic. Summers are hot and dry, and winters are cold everywhere, but rainfall decreases steadily proceeding east towards the Spanish border, from about 1,200 mm per year in the Baixo Corgo, to 850 mm in the Cima Corgo, and only 400 mm in the Douro Superior (marginal for grape growing).

The closest region to the Atlantic, the Baixo Corgo is the most fertile and abundant. It tends to produce the lightest wines (ruby and tawny Port), and accounts for about half of Port production. Cima Corgo is more than double in size, and is where most of the high quality tawny and vintage Port is made. Most of the famous producers are around the town of Pinhão. This region accounts for just over a third of all Port production. The Douro Superior is the largest of the three sub-zones, the most arid and the least developed.

The view from the river shows vineyards rising up with all angles of exposure, broken by woods where it was impossible to cultivate the land.

Only a small amount of Port is produced here, but it's become a focus for table wine production, because irrigation is permitted, and especially in conjunction with using vineyards at higher elevations, this allows the right degree of ripeness to be obtained.

Around Pinhão, the Douro is a monoculture, with vineyards rising up sharply on both sides of the river, broken only by some stretches of forest where the ground was just too difficult to create a vineyard. Vineyards line the valleys of the tributaries that feed into the Douro. They can face any angle, depending on the turns of the rivers, and may extend from close to the river to the peak of the hills. This creates significant variation. "This is mountain viticulture, but in some regions mountain viticulture is cool climate. The key feature of the Douro is that we are a hot climate. The three key factors in the Douro are the location, aspect, and altitude. The fourth factor is the cultivar," says António Magalhães, chief viticulturalist at Taylor Fladgate. "Temperature can decline about 2 degrees from vineyards at 100 m elevation to those at 400 m; and at the same hour of the day, at the same altitude, the difference between north-facing and south-facing vineyards is 2 degrees."

Vineyards are broken up, with around 34,000 farmers working around 142,000 individual holdings. Most growers have less than a hectare (often in multiple plots). The producers own about 5,000 ha, which form many of the larger vineyards among the total 45,000 ha. The gap between grape growers and wine producers has strong implications for the structure of the industry.

The Production of Port

Production of all Port starts in the same way, by adding spirits to stop fermentation, typically between a third and halfway through, when 5-6% alcohol has been produced. Enough spirit is added to bring the alcohol level over 16%. The sweetness of Port depends on just when the spirits are added during fermentation, although it's also possible to adjust sweetness by adding some very sweet wine at the end. The typical level of residual sugar is about 100 g/l residual sugar (a bit more than Sauternes or other dessert wines).

Color is important in Port. Whereas a conventional red wine may macerate with the skins for two or three weeks, all the color for Port must be obtained in the first 36-48 hours, before the spirits are added. The traditional means of extraction was to tread grapes by foot in a trough (a lagares). The romantic myth is that this method was developed as the perfect way for gentle extraction (the pips do not get crushed, for example), but of course it owes its development to the fact that there was no electricity to run equipment, while labor was cheap.

Most producers still use traditional foot-treading for the top Ports, but it's uneconomic for general production. However, most alternative methods for maceration are harsher. One of the best new systems is the robotic foot developed by Symington, which imitates the ability of the human foot to crush the grapes without squeezing the pips. Using lagares is really practical for only the high-end; cheaper Ports are made from grapes fermented in autovinification tanks, where the release of carbon dioxide is used to provide the

Symingtons use stainless steel lagares with mechanized silicon "toes" that mimic the treading action of the human foot.

energy source for maceration. (Autovinification was necessary originally because electricity was neither widespread nor reliable.)

The alcohol used for fortification comes in the form of aguardente, a spirit that legally must be 77% alcohol. The added volume is just over a quarter of the volume of the wine. Until recently, shippers were required to purchase the aguardente from distilleries elsewhere in Portugal; as this essentially came from distilling surplus wine, it was not necessarily of the highest quality. Many producers believe that a major improvement in the quality of Port occurred when they were allowed to choose their own sources of spirits. "I remember those Aguardentes, they used to be rustic, in your face, and it really marked the Port," says Sophia Bergqvist at Quinta de la Rosa.

"The spirits have a key role, not only in taking Port to 20%, but to balance the sweetness. This ensures the complexity and character but we don't want the spirits to give the character. We call this the quiet revolution because until 1991 we were forced to buy spirits

Traditional granite lagares have been modernized with heat exchangers and epoxy seals. They are used for the first three days of foot-treading, after which a robot (at the end) takes over.

from the state, and quality was average—it depended on the quality of wine that was distilled. When we were freed up to obtain other spirits, we could get very clean pure spirits. Vintage Port today is more approachable when young because the spirits are so much cleaner and purer that they allow the fruits to express themselves more," says David Guimaraens, chief winemaker at Taylor Fladgate. This is especially important for Vintage Port. "The purity of the spirits shows increasingly as Port ages. Lower quality spirits start to break down after five years or so," says Adrian Bridge. Some producers use different sources of spirits for different types of Port.

Once fermentation has been stopped, the wine is pressed off. A month later it is racked off the lees, and alcohol is brought up to around 20% if the level is below this. This is the point at which lots are selected for different types of Port. The transition from cask to bottle has always been a determinative event in Port, both commercially and stylistically. The basic issue is whether the wine

Grapes	$1.20
Aguardente	$0.60
Bottle	$0.50
Cork	$0.20

Grapes are the most expensive ingredient in Port, but Aguardente (brandy) is second, and a recent doubling in cost has put pressure on prices.

matures in bottle or in cask. The two extremes of each style are Vintage Port and Aged Tawny. Vintage Port is bottled after a short period of aging, at a point when its sheer power makes it undrinkable. It's likely to be held in large containers for the period before bottling. It matures in the bottle. Tawny Port may start off in large vats, but is transferred to Pipes (large barrels) for aging, and it stays in cask to a point at which it is ready to drink when bottled; the longer in spends in the cask, the higher the grade of Tawny. All the oak used in Port is old, of course.

Port is by far and away the most valuable wine produced in Portugal, but this disguises a multitude of sins. The most meaningful distinction is really between Ports where age is important and those where age is not significant. In the first category are vintage-style Ports (Vintage and LBV) and aged tawny Ports. This is the tail that wags the dog: only about 10% of sales, but producing roughly a third of the total annual revenue. Everything else is consumed in the relatively short term.

The vast majority of Port carries no vintage. It is blended from a variety of lots with the objective of maintaining consistency by evening out vintage fluctuations. Ruby Port is the simplest style, kept in large vats, often cement or stainless steel, for one year, and bottled

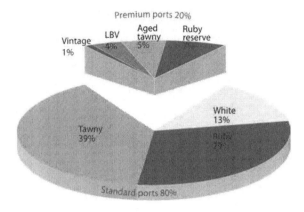

The Port Institute, the regulatory body, draws a distinction between standard Ports and premium Ports, with production running about 80% standard and 20% premium.

with an average age up to around three years. It's pretty powerful stuff. Ruby Reserve is aged a bit longer but isn't in principle much different. Tawny is supposed to be aged in wood until it's ready, but a standard Tawny may in fact be a lighter wine, adjusted for color and aroma. A Tawny Reserve must be aged for at least seven years.

Vintage Port and LBV

Vintage Port is the pinnacle of Port matured in the bottle. It is bottled after two or three years of aging in cask, and then is expected to take 15-20 years to mature. In some ways, this is the simplest Port to make, based on selecting the best lots in a top year, and bottling them in relatively short order.

Vintage Port is not made every year. Each Port shipper must decide within two years of the harvest whether that particular year will be high enough quality to be released as a Vintage Port. This is called "declaring the vintage." In a really great vintage, virtually every shipper will declare; in lesser vintages, those shippers who have done especially well, or who need a vintage perhaps because of past lack of success, will declare. On average, a shipper is likely to declare a vintage about three times a decade.

Port styles are divided according to whether the wine is matured in bulk or is bottled after brief cask aging in order to mature in the bottle.

Style	Aging
Matured in bulk	
Pink Port	Rosé, 6 months in vat
White Port	2-3 years in vat
Ruby	3 years in wood or steel
Ruby Reserve	4-6 years, mostly in barrique
Tawny	up to 6 years in barrique
Tawny Reserve	7 years in barrique
Aged Tawny	10, 20, 30, or 40 years in barrique
Colheita	7 years in barrique, from single vintage
Matured in bottle	
Crusted	2-3 years in cask, 3 years in bottle
Traditional LBV	4 years in cask then bottled
Single Quinta Vintage	single vineyard vintage, typically from nondeclared year
Vintage Port	2 years in cask

Vintage Port is deeply colored, and during its years in bottle, throws a massive sediment that requires decanting. It is a powerful wine, sweet, of course, with strong flavors of ripe black fruits. As it matures, the fruits lighten, as with any wine, and after fifty years or so it may even develop something of an overt impression of the spirits that were used to stop fermentation.

Until recently, Port was exclusively a blended wine, blended both from different grape varieties and from different vineyard sources. Since the 1980s, some single vineyard bottlings have appeared under the name of individual quintas (vineyards). Quinta is a slightly ambiguous term: nominally it means a vineyard, and can be used to identify the origin of a wine, but it is also used as the name for some famous producers, such as Quinta da Noval.

Unlike single vineyard wines in other regions, where the top vineyard in the top vintage is the best there is to offer, single quinta wines in Port are usually made in lesser vintages. In a great vintage, all of the wine is likely to go into the house's vintage Port. But in years just below the very top, when the vintage is not declared, the very best single vineyards may be worthy of bottling in vintage style. Taylor's Quinta de Vargellas is one of the best examples; the 1958 vintage started the trend. A single quinta Port is made in exactly the same way as a vintage Port, and usually has the compensating qualities of coming from the best vineyard but not the best year.

In recent years there has been something of a move towards producing single Quinta ports, partly from large producers in a move towards offering more variety at the highest quality levels, and partly from small, independent producers for whom it is their only product. When the rules for producing port were relaxed in 1986, some of the quintas that up to then had only sold grapes to larger producers began to produce and bottle their own wine. There are probably around fifty single Quinta ports today, roughly half coming from famous vineyards owned by large producers, and the other half representing new essays into the market from the owners. As a result, Port representing the vintage can now be found in most years.

The most famous single Quinta port is from Quinta da Noval; its top vineyard is called Nacional, and has been bottled separately for much longer than most single quinta Ports. Nacional is a small vineyard still containing ungrafted vines. Many people consider the 1931 Quinta da Noval Nacional to be the greatest Port of the twentieth century, although the 1931 vintage was not commonly declared.

Although Ports from single quintas are more common today, the driving force in Port remains blending. "We blend everything: location, aspect, altitude, cultivar," says António Magalhães at Taylor Fladgate. "Single quinta ports haven't succeeded," Rupert Symington says bluntly. "You would think that people would want to have a Port representing a particular place, but they don't, what they want is the brand, Dow or Grahams. And you can make much better Grahams by selecting the best lots rather than excluding some because they don't come from a particular source."

The rarity of vintage Port, usually with only two or three vintages declared each decade, has spurred lower-priced imitations. Most Port

The Nacional vineyard is small and the old vines are growing less vigorously.

in the vintage style carries a vintage, but Crusted Port, named because of the heavy deposit or crust that forms in the bottle, is a blend of wines from two or three vintages, aged in wood for two years like vintage Port, and then bottled.

At its best, LBV (late bottled vintage) can be a second wine that offers a good impression of vintage style, but a little less intense, and ready to drink sooner. A vintage not deemed good enough for a vintage Port will go into the making of a "traditional" LBV, which is left in wood for four to six years and then bottled. The extra time in cask makes the wine ready to drink, but it can still have a heavy sediment that needs decanting. LBVs originated during the 1950s, when the market was poor, and vintage Port would remain in cask beyond the usual limits while waiting for a buyer. The style was officially sanctioned in the 1960s.

The use of driven corks distinguishes the best LBVs from a lesser style of LBV, indicated by a stopper cork, where filtration and stabilization have removed all sediment to make the wine ready for immediate consumption. LBVs under stopper corks often enough are not much different from the better ruby Ports. The type of cork is the

Tawny Port and Colheitas age in old oak pipes after an initial period in larger wood vats.

best indication of style, but traditional LBVs also often state "unfiltered" on the label.

Aged Tawny Port

And now for something completely different. Tawny Port shows the same variety of quality and character as the range from Ruby to Vintage, but a different nature. Tawny Port gains its light color because it is matured in wood for several years, with the color lightening, and the flavor becoming drier and nuttier from oxidation. Evaporation during its maturation in wood increases the concentration of the wine.

Tawny Port with no indication of age is a staple of the industry, but not of much interest. Aged Tawny Ports are another matter. Tawny Ports can be labeled as 10, 20, 30, or 40 years, meaning that the wine has been aged in cask for that long. The age is the average of the wines that are blended, not an exact measure. Some houses

The Ramos Pinto blending room contains a large array of small bottles with samples of wines for blending. Ana Rosas calls this her piano.

can draw on stocks of wines going back for decades when they blend tawny port. "I really don't know how many different wines are blended into an aged tawny," says Ana Rosas, the master blender at Ramos Pinto. "It's too many to count and the amounts that are used vary widely." The skill is to maintain consistency of style with the same average age, but different wines each time there is a bottling.

There is a big jump in quality from non-aged Tawnies to 10-year Tawnies, and again to 20-year Tawnies. Gain in complexity as you go up to 30- and 40-year can be offset by an overblown quality resulting from oxidation. I find 20-year or 30-year to offer the most nuanced expression of the style, depending on the house. The aged Tawnies generally originate as blends of high quality wines from undeclared vintages, but distinguishing between the various ages is not just a matter of holding the wine longer in barrique. "To be able to produce 30 year Tawny, the starting wine needs to be vintage quality, to make a 10 year tawny requires wine that's LBV quality," explains winemaker Ricardo Pinto Nunes at Churchill.

Rather rare, but interesting when you can find it, is Colheita Port, which is a tawny from a single vintage. But remember that the significance of the vintage is the quality of the starting wine, with quality also influenced by the length of time in cask before bottling; little improvement occurs after bottling. Most houses produce Colheita occasionally, but some, like Kopke, specialize in them and may produce one in most years.

Ernest Cockburn, of the well-known Port house, once famously said that the first duty of a Port is to be red (the second is to be drunk), and in this context, the less said about white Port, which comes in varying levels of sweetness, the better. There are some exceptions in the form of aged white Ports, which tend to be a little livelier than their Tawny equivalents, because white grapes have higher acidity. Pink (rosé) Port is a recent development, intended to appeal to new consumers, made by running the wine off quickly (to minimize color), and bottling after a short period in vat.

Modernizing the Vineyards

The history of the vineyards still has an important effect on the character of Port. The original vineyards, many of which remain, have narrow terraces, often only one or two rows of vines wide, that curve and twist along the contours of the land. Varieties are intermingled, with many old vineyards containing 40 or more different varieties.

In 1983 the E.U. started a scheme to improve plantings in the Port region, with new plantings organized in blocks of each variety. Plantings were limited to five varieties. The replanting scheme has been a bit of a mixed bag, because the retaining walls between terraces were replaced by ramps to allow tractors to be used, but this requires the vines to be in more widely spaced rows on the broader terraces (called patamares). The lower density of planting makes the vines more productive. About half of the vineyards have now been replanted so they can be mechanized; the rest must be worked manually. On slopes below 35%, rows are sometimes planted going up the slope—called vertical planting in the region—so that tractors can go up and down, but erosion can still be a problem.

Traditional vineyards have narrow terraces following the contours of the land.

The changing character of the vineyards is a mixed blessing. "I don't agree with the subsidies for replanting the old vineyards. They should give subsidies for keeping them, they are the patrimony of the Douro, and they have many old varieties that will be lost if they are replaced," says Francisco Ferreira at Quinta da Vallado. There's recognition that it's important to maintain diversity. "When the vines planted in the seventies came to maturity, the wines did not have the complexity of the older types of varieties. We definitely pulled the bottom up, but we also pulled the top down. In the seventies and eighties, vineyards simplified, in the nineties they complexed back up," says David Guimaraes at Taylor Fladgate. "Today we actively plant 12 varieties, 4 are the majority and the others vary from location to location. In the past fifteen years we've recovered the old complexity, but instead of a field blend, we plant micro blocks."

The transition from intermingling varieties—what the French would call complantation—to planting in separate blocks has significant consequences for winemaking. Some producers believe it

New vineyards are made by carefully grading the land.

is a major advance; others see some advantages in the old system. "Vintage Port used to be made of grapes picked from field blends, so some were ripe and some were green. We're discovering the potential of the Douro only now, because now we're picking by variety, every grape is at perfection," says Rupert Symington. However, it's generally agreed that better results are obtained by fermenting the different varieties together. In Taylor Fladgate's new vineyards, "we pick multiple varieties at the same time and coferment them," says António Magalhães.

Getting grapes to more uniform ripeness, having temperature control in the lagares, and using spirits that are high quality all together may explain why Vintage Port now is much more approachable than before. It used to be that a Vintage Port had to be kept in bottle for ten or twenty years before you could even think of opening it; but today you are routinely offered the latest releases to taste, and they can be delicious (if still too overtly structured for my taste). It's becoming more a matter of personal taste whether you keep a vintage Port or drink it young, rather than necessity. "The ageability of Vintage Port is the same as it has always been, in fact it may be longer," says Rupert Symington.

The Dead Hand of the Beneficio

When Port production ran into difficulties in the 1930s, the *beneficio* system was introduced to limit production. The IVDP (Instituto do Vinho do Porto) sets a limit for the amount of wine that can be fortified to make Port. Wine in excess of the limit can be sold as dry table wine, but cannot be fortified. The total depends on the previous year's sales and the level of stocks held by the Port houses. It is apportioned among the growers on the basis of the classification of their vineyards. The beneficio states how maany grapes from each vineyard can be used to make Port.

Every vineyard is classified into one of six categories, labeled "A" through "F". 20% of the vineyards are graded A or B, and 5% are graded E or F. Classification factors include productivity (the lower the yield, the higher the mark), gradient (higher points for lower altitude), aspect, soil, exposure, and vine varieties. Each factor is given a numerical value, which is then tallied up. The amount of wine that can be used to make Port from any vineyard depends on its rating. When a grade A vineyard might be allowed to fortify 1,500 liters per hectare, a grade F would be limited to a third of that.

"The beneficio system is the last vestige of discredited 1930 economics. We're trying to run a business, but the system supposes we have a responsibility to support peasant farmers at subsistence level. We need to update the regulations to stimulate farmers who can produce quality grapes. This fundamentally has to change or the future of the industry is in question. My view is that the beneficio needs to be gone by 2020," says Adrian Bridges, managing director of Taylor Fladgate, a major group of Port houses.

The beneficio system evens out the level of Port production against the background of vintage fluctuation. Over the past twenty years, Port has averaged around 9 million cases per year. The proportion of wine allowed to be fortified is usually between a half and two thirds of production in the Douro. There is a big financial consequence, because grapes with a beneficio can sell for around 1000 per pipe (550 liters), whereas those without one (restricted to

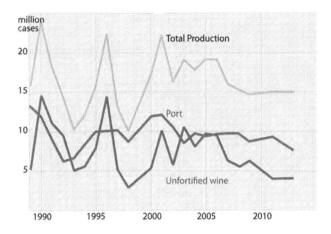

Port is more than half the production of the Douro. The volume of Port is about 79% wine and 21% added brandy. The volume of unfortified wine fluctuates more strongly with vintage.

making table wine) sell for about a third of the price. A free market would no doubt result in more fluctuation, but growers with lower quality vineyards would probably no longer see their prices artificially inflated by the beneficio. The Douro is an expensive place to grow grapes: it is economic for small farmers only because the beneficio inflates grape prices.

There is in a sense both over-supply and under-supply of grapes in the Douro. Over-supply is evidenced by the limitation on which grapes can be used to produce Port. Rupert Symington believes this should be dealt with by cutting out the D, E, and F vineyards. "Two thirds of the vineyards are really good quality (A, B, and C), but the other third could be pulled out," he says. Under-supply comes from the artificial inflation of grapes given the beneficio, which makes them too expensive to be profitable for producing table wine. This may be one factor in limiting the quality of table wine.

Shippers and Quintas

To say that production of Port is excessively regulated would be a mild expression of the exasperation felt by most producers. To be allowed to trade in grapes and wine, a shipper must have a minimum

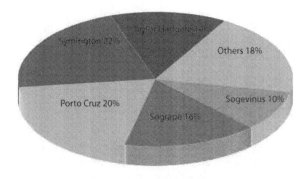

Five groups account for 82% of all port production. Symington and Taylor Fladgate are strong in premium ports. Sogevinus specializes in tawny ports (80% of their production). Porto Cruz produces only standard ports.

stock of 150,000 liters. This is a huge barrier to entry, and explains why Churchill Graham was the only new shipper to be founded in the past half century. (Remember that Port is based on trading: very few shippers rely solely on their own sources of production.)

Until the rules were liberalized in 1987, a lodge in Gaia was an absolute requisite for making Port. The change in the rules allowed individual producers to export directly from the Douro. This opened the way for bottlings from single quintas. However, the inability to purchase grapes or wine unless they meet the 150,000 stock minimum, coupled with the limitations of the beneficio system, effectively means they must rely exclusively on their own production. "It made sense 60 years ago, to stop Port shippers coming and going. But it doesn't make any sense today for people who own properties in the Douro," says Cristiano van Zeller.

So today there is a divide between two classes of producers. The shippers are based in Gaia, although a significant part of their activities has moved to the Douro. The quintas are based in the Douro, and since 1987, there has been a movement for quintas that used to sell grapes to the large shippers to produce their own Port. However, because of the limitations of the regulations, many of them have become focused more on producing table wine. The shippers have compensated for the loss of their sources by buying quintas when possible, but the possibilities for ownership are somewhat limited by the fragmentation of the vineyards.

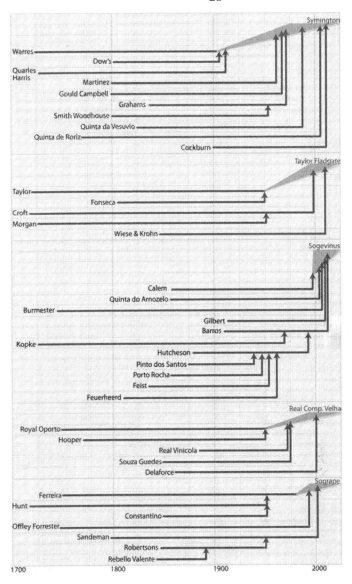

Mergers and acquisitions have brought most of the major port houses under the control of five groups. Port houses are placed from left to right according to date of founding. Vertical arrows show incorporation into other companies. Pink shading shows the period during which each group was assembled under its present ownership.

Port had a bad period in the 1940s and 1950s, when shipments were not much over two million cases per year, corresponding to less than 20% of production. (A fair amount of excess went into Mateus rosé, which was then becoming successful.) Many shippers went bust or merged. Spurred by the great 1963 vintage, recovery began in the sixties, but the consolidation of shippers has continued.

Although there has been increased concentration of the Port houses, they have mostly retained their individual reputations and styles. In the 1950s there were about 80 independent producers; today there are around 30. About 90 shippers are registered with the IVDP. There was a spate of purchases by international conglomerates in the 1970s and 1980s, but after 2000 most of them sold off the Port houses. This allowed some of the older houses to pick up the pieces, and now Port production is mostly concentrated into three large groups, Symington, Taylor Fladgate, and Sogrape. Symington and Taylor Fladgate each claim roughly 30% of the premium Port market; both are descendants of old British shippers, and the British influence remains strong; Sogrape is a large producer of wine in Portugal, with interests extending all over the country. Aside from a few houses owned by foreign owners (Sogevinus, owned by a Spanish bank is the largest), the remaining houses are independent, and mostly under Portuguese ownership.

The independence of each house within a major group is maintained by using specific sources (although sometimes a group will shift a quinta from one house to another). There can also be differences in the style of vinification, with some houses favoring a drier style than others.

The Future of Port

"What everyone wants to do with Port is to put it in the same pigeonhole as other sweet and fortified wines but I don't think that's fair. It's inaccurate to lump Port them together. Sales of all fortified wines (both Sherry and mutage) have declined sharply over 20 years (including Vermouth) but Port has been steady or increased," says Adrian Bridge at Taylor Fladgate. "The big trend in Port is that the top end is growing, and the commodity end is declining—and that will continue. It's a value game not a volume game."

La Martiniquaise built a new winery in 2014 with an annual capacity of 1 million liters for producing Porto Cruz. La Martiniquaise is France's second-largest spirits group and has owned Porto Cruz since 1972. In 2015 they purchased Quinta de Ventozelo, one of the largest quintas in the Douro, which originated in the 16th century.

The Port industry has tried hard to make its wine more attractive to new consumers, introducing Pink Port—"I invented Pink Port, it's a Port without rules," says Adrian Bridge—or proposing mixed drinks such as White Port with tonic, but "The Douro should focus on premium wines—without a doubt," says Rupert Symington. This accounts for only 20% of production, but a third of revenues, so that is still going to leave a lot of grapes going begging, and some revenues to make up. In the past, surplus grapes were sold off in bulk, but today there's a move towards making high quality table wines. Attitudes differ about this. "We know that the future is going towards table wine, the thing about the future is that we want to sell 50:50 table wines to Port," says Tania Oliveira at Sogevinus. Symingtons have an associated company, Prats & Symington that makes quality tables wines, although the scale is tiny compared with their Port production. "For me when we talk about the Douro valley we are talking about Port and not about table wine, because Port is a natural wine and table wine is not," says António Magalhães, explaining why he supports Taylor Fladgate's view that the company should stick to Port.

Red Wine in the Douro

"Table wine in the Douro twenty years ago was almost undrinkable, but now they have learned better viticulture and vinification. There has been a huge improvement on the wine making side, especially with the tannins," says Maria Campos at Churchill.

Portugal's first dry red wine with an iconic reputation, Barca Velha, came from the Douro Superior. When it was first produced by Port producer Ferriera in 1952, the use of methods from Bordeaux, such as fermenting in vats (instead of open lagares), pumping over the must, and applying temperature control (initially by a primitive system using blocks of ice brought up the river from Oporto), were major innovations for the Port region (resulting from a visit to Bordeaux by Ferreira's winemaker, Fernando Nicolau de Almedia).

Made from a Tempranillo-based blend consisting of Tinta Roriz, Touriga Nacional, Touriga Francesca, and Tinta Barroca, Barca Velha is produced only in the best years, only sixteen times to date. It is sold under the aegis of Casa Ferreirinha, the name used for the dry table wines from Ferreira, which is now part of Portugal's largest producer, Sogrape. Originally the wine was made at Ferreira's Quinta do Val do Me&ão, but Sogrape have now shifted production to Quinta da Leda, an estate in the same part of the Douro that they purchased in 1978. It's a sign of the revolutionary nature of making table wine in the Douro that it has taken fifty years for others to follow, although the styles are generally different.

As dry red wine was very much a second thought until recently, grape varieties grown in the Douro largely reflect their successfulness in Port. However, the varieties were distinguished systematically only in the 1980s. About 20 grape varieties are recommended for Port out of (probably) about 50 varieties growing in the region. Five varieties are considered to give the best Port. All are indigenous to Portugal, except for Tinta Roriz (a variant of Tempranillo).

Six major grape varieties total more than half of plantings		
Touriga Nacional	3%	Low yields give deeply colored and tannic wines. This is the top variety, considered to give the wines "grip."
Touriga Franca	22%	Good heat-resistance, does well in dry years, gives lighter wines than Nacional.
Tinta Roriz	12%	Variant of Tempranillo, gives firmness and length, does best in years that are not too hot.
Tinta Barroca	11%	Gives good color, structure, and body, with high sugar content.
Tinta Cão	5%	Low-yielding, intense flavor, is used for wines designed for long aging.
Tinta Amarela	5%	Not one of the recommended five varieties, but still widely grown, although difficult to get to ripeness.

It's surprising that Touriga Nacional, widely recognized as Portugal's best grape variety, is a relatively minor player according to the statistics. "A lot of Touriga Nacional has been planted in the Douro in the past ten years," says Francisco Ferreira at Quinta do Vallado, expressing scepticism about the official figures. One explanation for the figures may be that Touriga Nacional is difficult to grow. "People who make wine love Touriga, but not the viticulturalist because it's very hard work and very unproductive," says chief viticulturalist António Magalhces at Taylor Fladgate.

It is not axiomatic that varieties selected for making Port should be the best for making table wine. Douro DOC wines come only from indigenous varieties; international varieties can be used only for the lesser category of Vinho Regional. Perhaps for this reason, foreign varieties have not made much impact. "Mostly we use the traditional varieties, but we've tried other varieties; Cabernet Sauvignon doesn't work, but Syrah is good. It is not an authorized variety, but many people plant it and we'd like it to be authorized for the Douro," says António Agrellos, winemaker at Quinta da Noval." For table wine, I asked? "Why not for Port, it does well here." Labrador, a pure Syrah produced at Quinta da Noval, gives an impression somewhat reminiscent of the Northern Rhône.

"There is no Port variety I wouldn't recommend for Port, but there are varieties I wouldn't recommend for table wine," says Rupert Symington, who is making Chryseia, an iconic red wine at the Quinta de Roriz (converted from Port production). The varieties most suitable for making dry wine are Touriga Nacional, Touriga Franca, and Tinta Roriz (Tempranillo). Table wines mostly follow the model of Port in blending the varieties. The only one to have made inroads as a varietal in its own right is Touriga Nacional, which certainly has the strongest personality. Francisco Ferreira is enthusiastic about Touriga Nacional. "Some producers have reservations about Touriga Nacional, because they feel that too much dominates a blend. I don't agree because even if it does, it improves the quality."

Some producers have strong views about maintaining the tradition of blending. "Blends or varietals? Total blends, it's just not a question. The varieties developed here have been to make Port blends so they don't really make single varietals," says Sophia Bergqvist at Quinta de la Rosa. Indeed, monovarietals make it evident that Touriga Nacional is the most obviously structured of the varieties. The tradeoff between a Touriga Nacional varietal wine and a more conventional blend containing Touriga Franca ("Touriga Franca is our Merlot," says Rupert Symington) and other varieties is that Touriga Nacional shows great purity of fruit with a wonderful sense of precision; the blends are less precise but have broader flavors and greater generosity. I wouldn't say that one is better than the other; it's a matter of preference.

One distinctive feature of the production of table wines is that (black) grapes often start off in lagares like Port. "The difference in quality between using and not using lagares is enormous," says Cristiano van Zeller at Quinta Vale D. Maria. "Red wines go through 24-48 hours in the lagares before they go into the vats. You get more tannin, color, depth, but at the same time the tannins are velvety. In short the lagar gives greater intensity but also smoothness. Table wines are more approachable."

If there is a common feature to red table wine from the Douro, it is a combination of density and smoothness. Aside from the entry level wines, made in a fresh style to emphasize fruit, and offering very good value, Douro reds usually requires a bit of age. It's not so much that they are too tannic to drink when young, but there's a tendency for the black fruit aromatics to be muted on release, with a slightly flat impression on the finish; the aromatics get a bit of a lift after the first or second year in bottle, and the wines come more to life. For example, the 2014s almost all had a slightly flat edge to the finish in 2016, but the 2013 usually showed more lively aromatics.

It's dry and hot in Douro Superior, so it might seem counter-intuitive to base table wine production there. However, "The most important tables wines at Sogrape came from Douro Superior, so I know the area well, and I know that conditions are more reliable," says José Maria Soares Franco, who was in charge of production for the Douro at Sogrape from 1978 to 2006, and now has a new venture, Duorum, making table wine in the Douro Superior. " We can irrigate there (this requires an application to the authorities each year) and we harvest 2-3 weeks earlier, so there is less risk of rain at the equinox (generally a problem for Port). Keeping alcohol down is a good reason to go to Douro Superior."

It's somewhat of a surprise that the Douro can make white wines given its character as a hot climate. "The big revolution in the last ten years is not in the reds, it's in the whites," says Francisco Ferreira at Quinta do Vallado. "We've changed the varieties for whites from Port, of course, because we have the most fantastic set of varieties for reds, but among the whites most of the varieties used to make Port are not good for table wine, they were chosen to be very productive and to be very sweet, so we would need less brandy (brandy was expensive). So now we use varieties that are much more balanced with good acidity; of course we still have to pick at the right time."

White grapevines are usually planted at the highest altitudes in north-facing vineyards to maintain freshness, and producers say that they get enough natural acidity that they don't need to acidify. The whites can be fresh and crisp, sometimes with soft aromatics depending on the variety, and quite attractive for immediate consumption. They usually have quite moderate alcohol. The closest comparison that comes to mind is Muscadet. But although some producers say that the whites can age, I am sceptical, as I don't see the underlying basis for more flavor interest to develop (with some rare exceptions). Older whites seem to lose fruit rather than to gain complexity after the first two or three years.

Vintages

The top vintages in the past two decades are 2015(?), 2011, 2007, and 2000, but there have been many vintages without declarations that have made excellent single quinta Ports. In the 1990s, the outstanding vintages were 1997 and 1994. The years from 1975-1992 generally showed lower quality, as the unsettled situation in Portugal reflected itself in conditions for making Port. The best vintages in this period were 1985 and 1977. Before then 1970 and 1966 are very good, but outshadowed by the great, classic vintage of 1963, which is really the benchmark for the second half of the twentieth century. Before that, 1955, 1948, and 1945 are classic.

	The Twenty-First Century
2016	Unprecedented rain in spring and summer does not bode well.
2015 ***?	Universal enthusiasm for both Ports and red wines.
2014	Very difficult year due to rain throughout season.
2013	Dry summer and wet September, with few declarations
2012 *	Overshadowed by 2011, so few declarations.
2011 ***	A successful year with high quality Vintage and LBV, the best of the trio from 2011 to 2013
2010 *	A rainy year caused problems with ripening and lack of concentration.
2009 **	Very mixed, with opulent wines from some houses but no declarations from others.
2008 *	A second level year with some very good single quinta wines.
2007 ***	A great year, lovely purity to Vintage Ports.
2006 *	Rain in September limited good results to vineyards picking early.
2005 **	Drought kept yields down and made powerful wines.
2004 *	Good but not top year, with some excellent single quinta Ports.
2003 **	In spite of very hot conditions, most houses declared the vintage.
2002	Rain at harvest spoiled what would have been a good vintage.
2001 *	Higher yield year gave single quinta wines lighter style
2000 ***	Small harvest with almost universal declaration; deep and pure.

Visiting the Region

Port production is now more or less split between the Lodges in Vila Nova de Gaia and the quintas along the Douro. Within the space of a few hundred yards along the waterfront at Gaia, you can visit most of the important houses. Most have tasting rooms that you can walk into, but it can be very crowded in the summer season, and it is usually better to make an appointment.

Some of the houses now have visitor centers at their quintas in the Douro, and many of the quintas can be visited by appointment. Getting to the Douro is now simple by autoroute, although the most picturesque way to go remains the railway from Oporto station. However, it is difficult to rent a car in the Douro, so going by train (or boat) is an option only for visiting those quintas within easy reach of the station. Pinhão is the most central base for visiting the quintas of the middle Douro. The road along the Douro stops at Pinhão, so to the east of Pinhão, the train (which runs along the river) or boat are the only way to view the vineyards from the river. There is a spectacular road along Rio Torto, running south from Pinhão, if you have a car.

Small producers who do not belong to a major group usually have quintas only in the Douro, so this may be the only option to visit them. This is also where most table wine production occurs. There are fewer quintas to visit in the Douro Superior, which is less accessible, but Vila Nova de Foz Coã would be the best base (near the archeological park).

The maps show the locations of the shippers in Gaia and of the most important quintas in the Douro.

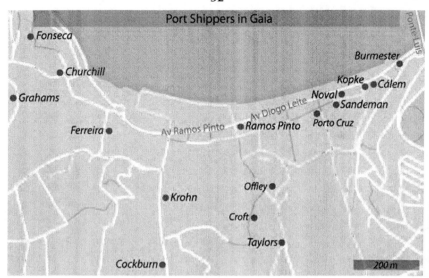

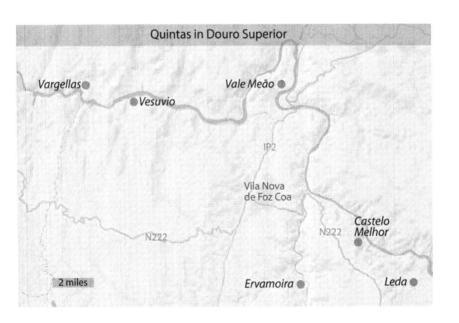

Producer Profiles

Ratings	
***	Excellent producers defining the very best of the appellation
**	Top producers whose wines typify the appellation
*	Very good producers making wines of character that rarely disappoint

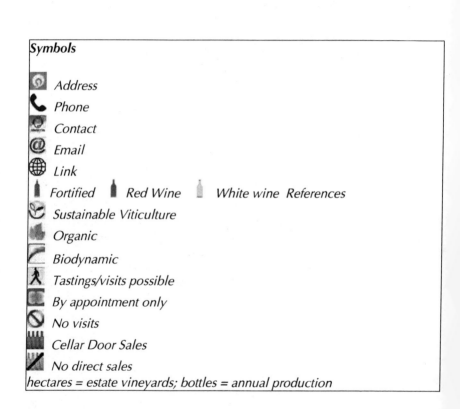

Symbols

Address
Phone
Contact
Email
Link
Fortified   Red Wine   White wine References
Sustainable Viticulture
Organic
Biodynamic
Tastings/visits possible
By appointment only
No visits
Cellar Door Sales
No direct sales
hectares = estate vineyards; bottles = annual production

Burmester

📍 *Rua Barão Forrester n° 73, 4000-034 Vila Nova de Gaia*

📞 *(351) 223 747 290*

@ *burma@jwburmester.com*

📸 *Tania Oliveira*

🌐 *http://www.burmesterporto.com*

🕯 *Colhieta, 1952*

🚶 🏭 G

Burmester & Nash started as a company trading cereals in London. After moving to Vila Nova de Gaia, it began shipping Port. The original company was replaced at the end of the eighteenth century by Burmester & Sons. The family members moved into banking in London, and the Port company was run by a distant relative, with the name changing again to J. W. Burmester in 1880. The company continued to be run by descendants of the family until it was sold to Amorim (the cork company) in 1999, who in turn sold it on to Sogevinus in 2005. Well known for its Colheitas, Burmester is the most elegant in style of the Ports in the Sogevinus portfolio. "It's more complex on the nose, the most feminine," says Tania Oliveira. Grapes come mostly from the Douro Superior. The 1952 Colheita may have been the most delicate Port I tasted during a recent visit to the Douro.

Cálem

 *Av. Diogo Leite, 26, 4400-111 Vila Nova de Gaia*

📞 *(351) 223 746 660*

@ *turismo@sogevinus.com*

Tania Oliveira

🌐 *http://www.calem.pt*

🍾 *Colheita, 1961*

🚶 🏭 G

50 ha; 2,000,000 bottles, 90% Port

Established by the Cálem family in 1855, Cálem became one of Portugal's leading brands under the original family ownership, and its Quinta da Foz was the backbone of some well regarded Vintage Ports in the post war years, although it ran into difficulties with quality in the eighties and nineties. Cálem became part of Sogevinus in 2003, but Quinta da Foz was not included. It was replaced as the main supply of grapes when Sogevinus bought Quinta do Arnozelo in the Douro Superior in 2004. Located by the bridge on the waterfront in Vila Nova de Gaia, its principal Lodge (there are others elsewhere in Gaia) is a major tourist attraction, receiving over 200,000 visitors a year. Its standard Tawny brand, Velhores, is well known in Portugal. The best wines coming from Cálem are the Colheitas.

Churchill Estates

CHURCHILL'S

LATE BOTTLED VINTAGE
PORT 2002

Rua da Fonte Nova, 5, 4400-156 Vila Nova de Gaia

(351) 223 703 641

office@churchills-port.com

Maria Campos

http://www.churchills-port.com

Vintage, 1997

Tawny, 20-year

Quinta de Gricha, 2007

50 ha; 240,000 bottles, 50% Port

"When Churchill's was founded in 1981, we were the first new Port shipper in fifty years," says Maria Campos, Churchill's CEO. "And since then, no new export company has been founded with cellars in Gaia." The driving force for the venture was Johnny Graham, a member of the Graham family who was not allowed to use his own name for the new company, so called it Churchill Graham (Churchill from his wife's family). Today it is called Churchill Estates. It started by purchasing grapes and making only Port, then in 1999 purchased the Quinta de Gricha (the first of five vineyard purchases). Since then, Churchill has produced table wine as well as Port, and today production is split more or less equally between the two. Tables wines and Ports are made at separate locations. Visitors come to a charming old house just off the waterfront, where there is an elegant tasting center. The approach to Port is distinctive. "Johnny has always had his own vision, his own sense of style. For example, everyone has young white Port, but he introduced a ten year old white Port. The wines have a lot of personality. They are sweet but not too sweet, not as sweet as some, they have power but it's restrained with elegance. An important feature is the natural acidity which gives good balance. They have a backbone, we always say we like wines with tension," says Maria. Indeed, the house style for both red Douro wines and Ports shows that thread of acidity supporting an impression of minerality. The white port is aged for ten years, and although described as a dry aperitif, this is relative to Port (it has 60 g/l) but the style is quite crisp and appley. Tawnies are dark with a luscious impression; the vintage port brings out to the full the refined style of the house, with well delineated fruits giving almost an impression of minerality. Because the house is young, there are only 10- and 20-year Tawnies at the present, but a 30-year is about to be introduced. As the dry red wines develop, overt fruits give way to a more savory impression. This is reinforced in the Touriga Nacional compared with the Gran Reserva blend, but all show a nice sense of mineral precision. Quinta de Gricha is softer and more aromatic. This is an unusual house that puts equal energy into table wines and Ports, and produces both with the same high quality and original character.

Cockburn

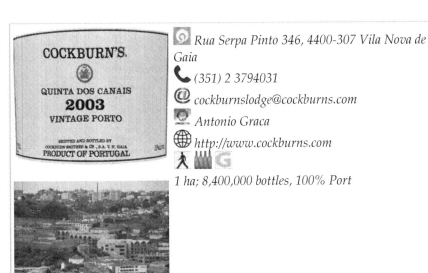

COCKBURN'S.

QUINTA DOS CANAIS
2003
VINTAGE PORTO

SHIPPED AND BOTTLED BY
COCKBURN SMITHES & Co., S.A. V.N. GAIA
PRODUCT OF PORTUGAL

Rua Serpa Pinto 346, 4400-307 Vila Nova de Gaia

(351) 2 3794031

cockburnslodge@cockburns.com

Antonio Graca

http://www.cockburns.com

1 ha; 8,400,000 bottles, 100% Port

Cockburn's is a demonstration of the dangers of conglomerates. Founded by Robert Cockburn from Scotland in 1815, it continued under family ownership, with a change of name to Cockburn Smithies in 1845, reflecting a partnership with the Smithies family. In 1962, it was sold to Harvey's of Bristol. Harvey's then became part of Allied Domecq. When Allied Domecq was taken over by Pernod Ricard, Cockburn's was sold to Fortune Brands (the owners of the Beam spirits company). Finally in 2010, Cockburn's was sold to Symington, its first owners in half a century who know anything about Port. During the seventies and eighties, its corporate owners bought several quintas in the Douro, ensuring sources of supply. Quinta dos Canais, which was added in 1989, makes a single quinta Vintage Port in undeclared years. Some of its former quintas have been taken over by Symingtons to supply other houses, most notably Quinta de Tua, which is now part of Grahams. In spite of the investments, the wines went through a fairly rough period under the various owners; the question now is not so much whether the Symingtons can re-establish Cockburn at the highest level, but what sort of style they will follow as they do so.

Croft Port

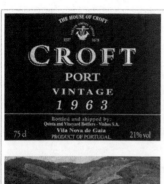

🔲 *Rua Barão de Forrester, 412, 4400-034 Vila Nova de Gaia*
& Quinta da Roêda, Pinhão

📞 *(351) 223 755 514*

@ *turismo.roeda@croft.pt*

🌐 *http://www.croftport.com*

🍷 *Vintage, 2011*

🚶 🏭 **G N**

109 ha; 20,000,000 bottles, 100% Port

Croft is a very old producer, dating from 1558, but has had its ups and downs in the past few years. It's one of the old British shippers; the first Croft joined as a partner in 1736. In 1889 it acquired Quinta da Roêda, in Pinhão, which became the heart of its Vintage Port. Today it also houses the Croft Visitor Center (a short walk from the train station). The spirits company, Gilbey's, purchased Croft in 1911, in the 1970s it extended its activities to Sherry, and then Croft became part of the international conglomerate Diageo when they purchased Gilbey's. It is fair to say that Croft did not prosper under Diageo; the Vintage Ports were no longer regarded as leading lights. In 2001, Croft was purchased by Taylor Fladgate (its interests in Sherry were sold to Gonzales Byass and Croft Brandy stayed with Diageo), and a revival began. Croft had ceased to make its Vintage Port in the traditional lagares by foot-treading after the 1963 vintage, but with the 2003 vintage, traditional methods were reintroduced. Now parts of Quinta da Roêda have been replanted. Croft is in a sense the bottom tier of the quality arm of Taylor Fladgate, still ranking below Taylor and Fonseca; it is fair to say that its Vintage and Tawny Ports are less sophisticated. It is also notable as the origin of Pink Port. This is effectively a sort of rosé, produced on a much more rapid timescale than traditional Port, intended to introduce new consumers to Port as an aperitif.

Dows Port

Apartado 26, P-4401 Vila Nova de Gaia
(351) 237 776 300
symington@symington.com
http://www.dows-port.com

35 ha; 10,000,000 bottles, 100% Port

Dow's is one of the trio of major houses in the Symington portfolio. Founded in 1798 when Bruno da Silva, a Portuguese merchant from Oporto, started importing Port to London, it was known as Silva & Cosens until the firm merged with the much smaller house of Dow in 1877. Symingtons have been partners in the firm since 1912, and it became part of their group in 1961. Dow Ports are made in a slightly drier style than most, and there is a full range from Vintage to Ruby. The most important component in the Vintage comes from Quinta da Bomfim, facing south over the Douro at Pinhão. Another important source used to be Quinta da Senhora da Ribeira, but Dow's had to sell it in 1954 during financial difficulties; however, it was repurchased in 1998.

Duorum

Quinta de Castelo Melhor, EN 222, Km 216.8, 5150-146 Vila Nova de Foz Côa

@ duorum@duorum.pt

Vera Magalhães

http://www.duorum.pt

Reserva, 2012

126 ha; 200,000 bottles, 10% Port

The Duorum project tries to make world-class wine all over Portugal from Alentejo to Vinho Verde. It's a medium size group with about 10 million bottles total; the Douro provides about 1.5 million. The winery and vineyards in the Douro were established in 2007 by João Portugal Ramos and José Maria Soares Franco, at Quinta Castelo Melhor in the Douro Superior (the hottest and driest part of the region), close to the Spanish border, where they have bought land extending from 130-450 m altitude. José Maria was in charge of production at Sogrape (Portugal's largest wine company) from 1978 to 2006. It's dry and hot in Douro Superior, so it might seem counter-intuitive to base table wine production there. However, "The most important tables wines at Sogrape came from Douro Superior, so I know the area well, and I know that conditions are more reliable. We can irrigate there (this requires an application to the authorities each year) and we harvest 2-3 weeks earlier, so there is less risk of rain at the equinox (generally a problem for Port). Keeping alcohol down is a good reason to go to Douro Superior. We think that more than 13.5% kills the aromas and quality of the wine, this is very important in our style." Duorum is producing mostly table wine, with a range of about 9 wine, including Tons (an entry level wine), Colheita (not a Port in this context), a Reserva, and O. Leucura (a play on words which loosely means astonishment, and is a top flight wine in the European tradition). All the table wines are blends; "We find in each variety something that adds to our character. We use only indigenous varieties, we think consumers will get tired of the similarities of wines made everywhere from Cabernet Sauvignon and Syrah" The high level wines come only from estate grapes, but grapes are purchased for the entry level wines. White wine is about a quarter. "In white wines we look for a strong intense aroma, floral character, with good acidity.," says José Maria. "In reds the style is to have a deep color, good structure, intense character, and fruitiness. For that reason we use the two Touriga varieties, Nacional and Franca. We want to get ripe tannins, that is why we go to the Douro Superior." The style has dense fruits and tannins on the palate, but the tannins are not aggressive and have that softness produced by extraction in lagares. All the same, I would give two or three years in bottle before expecting the variety of fruit flavors to come out. Port is a small part of production, with both LBV and vintage Port. In a couple of years there will be a 10-year Tawny and a Colheita.

Fonseca

★★★

🄾 *Rua Rei Ramiro, 357, 4400 Vila Nova de Gaia*

📞 *(351) 223 719 999*

@ *marketing@fonseca.pt*

🌐 *http://www.fonseca.pt*

🍷 *Guimaraens, Vintage, 2013*

🍷 *Tawny, 20-year*

🚶 ▦ G N

106 ha; 3,400,000 bottles, 100% Port

It's often a tossup whether to prefer Fonseca or Taylor in vintages that both have declared. It's really a matter of which style best suits the vintage: Taylor's ineffable elegance or Fonseca's slightly greater sense of power. Fonseca dates from the purchase of pipes of Port by Santos Fonseca in 1815; then the company was bought by Manuel Pedro Guimaraens in 1822. Today it is part of Taylor Fladgate, and David Guimaraens is the winemaker for the whole group (including the major houses of Taylor, Fonseca, and Croft). In vintages that Fonseca does not declare, there may be a single vineyard port made from Quinta do Panascal (which Fonseca purchased in 1978), but the Guimaraens Vintage is probably better known; this is a blend from all three vineyards (including Santo António and Quinta do Cruzeiro near Pinhão) that would go into Fonseca when a vintage is declared, so it's a second wine, representing the best lots in an undeclared year rather than the second best lots in a declared year. The 20-year Tawny is elegant but luscious. Fonseca is well known also for Bin 27, a very successful Reserve Ruby Port (one of the few that can be recommended at this level), which maintains a consistent level of quality.

Graham ★★★

 *Travessa do Barão de Forrester, 86, 4400 Vila Nova de Gaia*

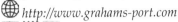 *(351) 223 776 300*

grahams@grahams-port.com

http://www.grahams-port.com

70 ha; 6,000,000 bottles, 100% Port

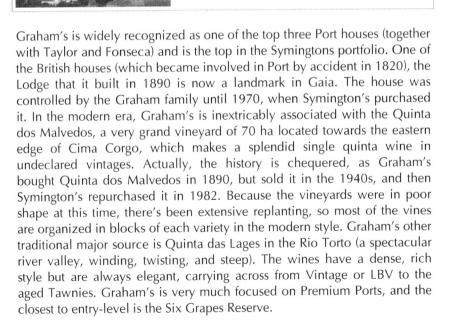

Graham's is widely recognized as one of the top three Port houses (together with Taylor and Fonseca) and is the top in the Symingtons portfolio. One of the British houses (which became involved in Port by accident in 1820), the Lodge that it built in 1890 is now a landmark in Gaia. The house was controlled by the Graham family until 1970, when Symington's purchased it. In the modern era, Graham's is inextricably associated with the Quinta dos Malvedos, a very grand vineyard of 70 ha located towards the eastern edge of Cima Corgo, which makes a splendid single quinta wine in undeclared vintages. Actually, the history is chequered, as Graham's bought Quinta dos Malvedos in 1890, but sold it in the 1940s, and then Symington's repurchased it in 1982. Because the vineyards were in poor shape at this time, there's been extensive replanting, so most of the vines are organized in blocks of each variety in the modern style. Graham's other traditional major source is Quinta das Lages in the Rio Torto (a spectacular river valley, winding, twisting, and steep). The wines have a dense, rich style but are always elegant, carrying across from Vintage or LBV to the aged Tawnies. Graham's is very much focused on Premium Ports, and the closest to entry-level is the Six Grapes Reserve.

Kopke

📍 *Av. Diogo Leite, 4400-111 Vila Nova de Gaia*
📞 *(351) 223752420*
@ *turismo@sogevinus.com*
💬 *Tania Oliveira*
🌐 *http://www.sogevinus.com/kopke*
🕯 *Colheita, 1941*
🕯 *White Port, 30-year*

🚶 🏰 G

360 ha

Kopke was established in 1638 by Christiano Kopke and his son Nicolau, who came to Portugal from Germany. Kopke became part of Barros in 1953, and then joined the Sogevinus portfolio when Sogevinus bought Barros in 2006. Kopke is famous for its Colheitas. Its main source of supply comes from Quinta de São Luiz (facing north across the Douro, a few miles to the west of Pinhão), which was purchased in 1922. This is now an important center of vinification for Sogevinus. Kopke is always a blend from low altitude vineyards (to give concentration) and high altitudes (to give freshness). Kopke's main focus is on Colheitas —in principle they are prepared to produce one every year—but they are unusual also in producing 10, 20, 30, and 40-year white Ports. "There's a difference in production from aged Tawnies, because the whites are more delicate; we have to add the brandy in stages instead of all at once or we lose some phenolics. The cellar for aging white Ports is fresher by one or two degrees and it's harder than making Tawnies because oxidation can spoil them more easily. A specialized team looks after the whites," explains Tania Oliveira. "At the moment, one of our difficulties is to get really good white grapes in the Douro," she says, "so Quinta do Bairro (near Régua) has been converted to white grape varieties to ensure the supply for White Port."

Production of aged Tawnies and Colheitas is based on an extensive supply of old stocks; there is a 1935 Colheita that is still in cask and bottled on demand. The 1941 is fresh today; it would have been a field blend, probably including white grapes, which may be why it has stayed so fresh. With lots of character, the wines are quite distinct.

Niepoort ⋆⋆

📍 *Rua Cândido dos Reis, 598, 4400-071 Vila Nova de Gaia*

📞 *(351) 222 001 028*

@ *info@niepoort-vinhos.com*

🖥 *Susana Ferez*

🌐 *http://www.niepoort-vinhos.com*

🍾 Redoma

🍷 Redoma

🍷 G

103 ha; 600,000 bottles

Niepoort is one of the few remaining independent Port shippers. Originating when the Niepoorts arrived from Holland in 1842, it remains in the hands of the fifth generation of the family today. Joining the company in 1987, Dirk Niepoort has been the driving force behind an expansion into owning vineyards and producing tables wines as well as Ports. Originally all grapes came from growers, but Quinta de Nápoles was purchased in 1988 (and is now the headquarters), followed by Quinta do Carril in 1989 and Quinta do Passadouro in 1990. There's a very wide range of Ports, with the entrepreneurial spirit showing in a Garrafeira (produced in glass demijohns), a 10-year white Port, as well as many Tawnies, a Crusted, Colheitas, and various Vintage Ports. Niepoort also sells an Aguardente brandy. Production of table wine started with the Redoma red in 1991, and the Redoma white followed in 1993. Coming from altitudes over 400 m, and balanced between savory and fruit, Redoma is one of the few Douro whites that ages well. A new top-level red wine, Batuta, was introduced from Quinta do Carril; this is a much bigger wine compared to Redoma's relative tightness. Besides the Douro, Niepoort has expanded into other regions in Portugal, collaborating with winemakers in the Dão and Vinho Verde, as well as ventures elsewhere in Europe

Quinta do Noval ★★

Av. Diogo Leite, 256, 4400 Vila Nova de Gaia
& Quinta da Noval, Pinhão
(351) 223 752 020
noval@quintadonoval.pt
Ana Carvalho
http://www.quintadonoval.com
Vintage, 2013
Colheita, 2000
Labrado,r 2012
145 ha; 500,000 bottles, 70% Port

Quinta do Noval is perched right at the top of one of the tiny roads out of Pinhão. Approaching the winery, you pass a long series of old stone walls going up to carefully tended terraces. These occupy about a third of the vineyards, with only a couple of rows on each terrace, and require continuous maintenance. "It's more work than the pyramids," says winemaker António Agrellos. There are 100 ha planted in this estate of 145 ha, and more vineyards across the Douro. Just below the winery is the famous Nacional vineyard, a tiny plot of 1.7 ha where the vines are still on their original roots. Planted in 1924, the vineyard contains a mix of many varieties; when a vine dies, it is replaced by one of the same variety to maintain the complexity of the field blend. Many people consider Nacional 1931 to be the best Vintage Port of the twentieth century. Under the ownership of the van Zeller family from the late nineteenth century, Quinta do Noval had a distinguished history of innovation, developing aged Tawnies, and introducing LBV as a new category in 1958. When the laws were liberalized, it was one of the first to transfer all production to the quinta in the Douro. (It still has premises on the waterfront in Gaia, where there is a tasting room.) As the result of family problems, it was sold in 1993 to AXA Millésimes, the wine investment arm of AXA insurance (who also own châteaux in Bordeaux, a domain in Burgundy, and wineries in other places). Innovation has continued. Noval started to make table wine in 2000. "When we took over, Noval had 60-70 ha and much was not in good condition, so we didn't have enough grapes to join the revolution and produce table wine, but we have planted and now we have enough. Mostly we use the traditional varieties, but we've tried other varieties; Cabernet Sauvignon doesn't work, but Syrah is good," says António. Wines come from both estate and purchased grapes. Noval on the label means the grapes are purchased. "Whenever we put Quinta do Noval on the label, all the grapes come from the estate," explains António. Both Ports and table wines show a clean style emphasizing purity of fruits, elegant and taut. Of recent vintages ("Our objective is to make vintage every year, not just when there is a general declaration.") the 2013 is the most approachable. In aged Tawnies, Noval produce 10, 20, and 40-year, but the Colheita 2000 is wonderfully delicate right now. Table wines are a mix of Douro DOC using traditional varieties and Vinhos Regional using new varieties, including Labrador (a 100% Syrah). It's hard to go wrong here.

Prats & Symington

Quinta de Roriz, São João da Pesqueira, 5130-113 Ervedosa do Douro

☎ 022-3776300

@ info@chryseia.com

Rupert Symington

⊕ http://www.chryseia.com/

🍷 Chryseia

Quinta de Roriz is the center of Prats & Symington, founded by Rupert together with Bruno Prats (formerly of Château Cos d'Estournel in Bordeaux) on a somewhat ad hoc basis in 1998 to produce table wines in the Douro. (Previously it was used to produce single quinta Port by Kopke, then later the grapes were used by Ferreira and Quinta da Noval.) Starting by purchasing grapes, and releasing the first vintage in 2000, the project proved so successful that they bought their own vineyards, most notably Quinta de Roriz in 2009. Other sources include Quinta da Perdriz in the Rio Torto. The dilapidated buildings at Roriz are being restored and extended and all the wines are now made here in what will become a modern winery. The vineyards are being regraded and planted with the varieties most suitable for making table wine, which means Touriga Nacional and Touriga Franca. Touriga Nacional gives structure and breed, softened by Touriga Franca ("Touriga Franca is our Merlot," Rupert says). Three wines come from Quinta de Roriz. The top wine, Chryseia, shows what the Douro can do in the way of a wine that will compete in the international area, and has rapidly become one of Portugal's iconic table wines. "It's a real vin de garage; it's a microscopic operation," comments Rupert. Post Scriptum (a clever name) is a second label, introduced in

2002, roughly an equal blend of lots that were matured in new oak but which weren't ultimately used for Chryseia, and lots that were set aside at the outset to be matured in two year oak. "Post Scriptum is very much a second wine of Chryseia," Rupert says, "we don't say a lot will be one or the other until a final tasting." Prazo de Roriz is a third wine based on the varieties that don't make the cut for Postscriptum and Chryseia. The objective with these wines is to get purity of expression. "I think Douro wine is all about purity of fruit," Rupert says. "There's no Portiness. It would be easy to get lots of extraction and alcohol, but that's not what we want." Chryseia and Post Scriptum rest in new oak for 15 months, Prazo de Roriz for less time. The style is modern, clean and pure, with Chryseia definitely showing a greater generosity of fruits than Post Scriptum. A lovely structured backbone should ensure longevity.

Ramos Pinto **

 Av. Ramos-Pinto, 380, Apartado 1320, 4401-997 Vila Nova de Gaia

📞 *(351) 223707000*

@ *jrosas@ramospinto.pt*

📷 *Ema Rodriguez*

🌐 *http://www.ramospinto.pt*

🍾 *Tawny, 20-year*

🍾 *Quinta do Bom Retiro, Vintage, 2014*

🚶 🏭 G

239 ha

Located right on the waterfront, Ramos Pinto has an old house that's now a visitor center and museum (where they show the risqué posters on which the company built its advertising early in the twentieth century). Further up the hill, safely away from the floods that used to happen, are extensive cellars. Founded by Adriano Ramos Pinto in 1880, the house remained under the same family ownership until it was sold to Champagne Roederer in 1990. However, it is run today by master blender Ana Rosas, the fifth generation of the founding family, and still regards itself as a small producer. Ports and table wines (produced in roughly equal proportions) come only from estate grapes. The most important of its four estates are Bom Retiro, in Cima Corgo, and Ervamoira in Douro Superior (which provides three quarters of production). Ramos Pinto has long been known for the quality of their Tawny ports. "Tawny really is the soul of Port, it's what the house is about, it's how we have learned to age the wines, it's the style of the house," says Ana. There isn't a single style because the 10-year and 20-year come from different vineyards, the 10-year from Ervamoira, the 20 year from Bom Retiro. As a result, the ten year shows all the power of the Douro Superior, the hottest and driest part of the region; in fact, the average age is between 12 and 13 years because the wines are initially so intensely colored that they take longer then ten years for the color to attenuate to the point at which the wine can be approved for Tawny port. It's still quite dark for a Tawny. The twenty year expresses the full delicacy and nuance of the aged Tawny style. The 30-year Tawny shows more concentration and intensity than the 10-year or 20-year, with a style that's between them in terms of the balance between power and elegance, as it's a blend from both Ervamoira and Bom Retiro, and the other vineyards. The focus of the house is very much on blending. How many different lots are blended into each Tawny? "I really don't know," Ana says, "it's too many to count and the amounts that are used vary widely." In the tasting room, there's a large array of small bottles with samples of wines for blending. Ana calls this her piano.

Quinta de la Rosa

Gouvães do Douro, 5085-215, Pinhão

(351) 254 732 254

quintadelarosa@quintadelarosa.com

Sophia Bergqvist

http://www.quintadelarosa.com

LBV, 2011

La Rosa, 2012

72 ha; 280,000 bottles, 33% Port

Sophia Bergqvist's great grandfather was a port shipper, and Quinta de la Rosa was given to her grandmother as a present in 1906. Financial difficulties caused the shipper to be sold in the thirties, but the family kept the quinta and sold the grapes to Sandeman. In 1988, when the laws for production of Port were liberalized, Sophia and her father decided to make their own Port. "We were one of the first to take advantage of the new regulations," she says. "And then in the 1990s we were one of the first to go into red table wine. The initial driving force was an excess of grapes that couldn't be used for Port." The red was sold as a house wine to Berry Bros. Today production is two thirds wine (mostly red) to one third Port. Grapes are purchased (especially for entry level wines) to supplement sources from the estate. The winery was built in 2012, and now there's also a guest house with 19 rooms attached to the winery. The vineyards run along the river, rising from the river to 450 m. There's no assignment of vineyards to purpose in advance, it depends on the year, although there are vineyards that do tend to make specific wines. The first winemaker was David Baverstock, an Australian, and the style was more exuberant with some American oak used during maturation. Jorge Moreira became the winemaker in 2002, and since then the quinta has moved to a more restrained European style. Sophia describes her aim for tables wines as "to maintain balance and equilibrium, not to over-extract. It's terribly important to control acidity because otherwise we end up with Port-like dry wines. The style of the Douro is fruit-driven wines with the minerality we get from schist soils, using old oak and not new oak." In Port, the house style goes for precision, you might almost say tight, with a sense of mineral restraint to the finish.

Taylor ***

Rua do Choupelo, 250, 4400 Vila Nova de Gaia

(351) 223 719 999

@ general@taylor.pt

⊕ http://www.taylor.pt

Tawny, 30-year

Quinta de Vargellas, Vintage, 2012

大 ⼭ G N

347 ha; 8,000,000 bottles, 100% Port

Taylor's is the jewel in the crown of Taylor Fladgate, a group that also holds Fonseca and Croft's. Dating from 1692, with the Quinta de Vargellas vineyard (just over the border in the Douro Superior) at its heart, Taylor Vintage is generally regarded as a sublime Port, one which together with Fonseca (also owned by Taylor Fladgate) and Graham's (owned by Symington's) defines the highest level of Port. Vargellas was purchased by Taylor's in 1893, a strong move as the vineyards were in the throes of phylloxera, but by 1908 the grapes were included in the Vintage Port. Taylor is the Rolls Royce of Port, always elegant, never heavy, yet always with that silky sense of power in the background. In years when Taylor does not declare a vintage, there is often a single quinta wine from Vargellas. There is a range of Tawny Ports, including 10, 20, 30, 40-year; for my money, the 30-year just edges out the 20-year as the finest of the range. There's also what amounts to a 50-year, in the form of a Tawny coming from a single vintage from the harvest fifty years ago. It's closer in style to the 30-year than to the 40-year, and is extraordinarily fine. This year's release is the 1966. This is essentially a 50-year-old Colheita (a Tawny from a single vintage), but "we don't use Colheita because no one knows what it means and no one can pronounce it," explains Marketing Manager Chris Forbes. so it's described as a single harvest. The Vintage and Aged Tawnies are really at the top of the game.

Quinta Vale D. Maria **

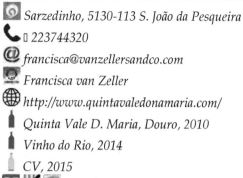

Sarzedinho, 5130-113 S. João da Pesqueira

☎ 223744320

@ francisca@vanzellersandco.com

👤 Francisca van Zeller

🌐 http://www.quintavaledonamaria.com/

🍷 Quinta Vale D. Maria, Douro, 2010

🍷 Vinho do Rio, 2014

🍷 CV, 2015

45 ha; 210,000 bottles, 15% Port

The Van Zeller family has a long involvement in Port, owning the eponymous shipper and Quinta da Noval until they were sold in 1993 as the result of problems in the family. Cristiano van Zeller started making wine at Quinta Vale D. Maria in 1996. It has been in his wife Joana's family for several hundred years, and had been leased out. "It was a complete ruin, with 10 ha of old vineyards, which have 41 varieties. We've grown to 45 ha, either purchased or leased, and I planted 5 ha of new vineyards between 2004 and 2007." In an obscure location off the Rio Torto (the local authority removed all the signs to the quinta that Cristiano had erected), the winery is the middle of the vineyards at about 200 m elevation. There's a mixture of granite lagares and stainless steel fermentation vats, but the plan is to replace the vats with more lagares as Cristiano feels this gives more subtle results in the wine. "You get more tannin, color, depth, but at the same time the tannins are smooth and velvety. Tables wines are more approachable." Cristiano managed to get back the name of van Zellers in 2006 when it had become more or less moribund, and this is now his negociant arm, making wines from purchased grapes. Production is focused on table wines, both white and red, but there is also a range of tawny and vintage Ports. Vale D. Maria makes entry level reds and whites (Rufo), two higher level wines, and four single vineyard wines. "So I'm identifying many different parcels that make distinct wines. A few parcels are dedicated to Port, everything else is for Table wine." Cristiano makes a set of about 10 wines for van Zeller. The quinta makes LBV and Vintage Port, and van Zellers has managed to obtain some old wines to produce aged Tawnies. The one word I would use to describe the wines is sophisticated. Displaying silky textures, the whites have a definite trend towards minerality, especially when you go above entry level. The reds are elegant and silky with a lovely sense of precision to the black fruits on the palate. Although alcohol is high, it's never evident on the palate. The style is subtle. Several vintages of the eponymous wine, labeled just Quinta Vale D. Maria Douro, which comes from the center of the quinta, reinforced my impression that it's a mistake to drink the red wines soon after release, because with an additional year or so, the aromatics really come to life. The single vineyard wines show the properties of different blends and locations, from Vinho de Francisca (named for Cristiano's daughter who now works with him) to Vinho do Rio, which comes from the lowest altitude vineyards, close to the river, and offers the most dense impression of all.

Quinta do Vallado

5050-364 Peso da Régua

(351) 254 323 147

geral@quintadovallado.com

Francisco Ferreira

http://www.quintadovallado.com

Tawny, 20-year

Reserva, 2013

Touriga Nacional, 2014

100 ha; 900,000 bottles, 5% Port

Francisco Ferreira is an enterprising fellow. Quinta do Vallado has belonged to his family for almost two centuries. It provided grapes for the family Port house, but was not included when Port Ferreira was sold to Sogrape in 1987. Francisco has been building up the quinta as an independent business since then, acquiring another quinta in the Douro Superior, and expanding into a chic boutique hotel that now sits besides the new winery at Vallado. There are 75 ha of vineyards in a more or less in a contiguous block around the winery, extending from 80-370 m, and another 25 ha at Quinta do Orgal in Douro Superior (where he also has another small hotel). Typical of the new independent producer in the Douro, production of table wine is greater than Port. As much of the Port isn't commercialized, it amounts to only about 5% of sales. Francisco produces both varietal wines and blends. All the wines are Douro DOC because all the varieties are indigenous. What are the stylistic objectives? "For whites and rosés, wines with some minerality, of course showing fruit, but acidity is important. We could have more structure but then we'd lose some freshness. For me Tawny Port must have complexity, of course, but it must have acidity." There's constant experimentation, with a dry white from Muscat as well as conventional blends. Reds focus on the local varieties, but there are monovarietal wines as well as blends. The style of both whites and reds is in the direction of elegance rather than power. The table wines are divided into three ranges. The entry level range is described as "Vallado" on the label, meaning that grapes have been purchased. The intermediate range, described as "Quinta do Vallado" to emphasize that grapes come from the estate, includes a white Reserva and two red varietal wines, Sousão and Touriga Nacional. Francisco is enthusiastic about Touriga Nacional. "Some producers have reservations about Touriga Nacional, because they feel that too much dominates a blend. I don't agree because even if it does, it improves the quality." The top range consists of a Reserva that's a field blend from 45 varieties of vines more than a hundred years old, and the Adelaide blend. also from very old vines. Adelaide is named for Francisco's ancestor, Dona Antonia, who built up the business in the nineteenth century. In Ports, which are something of a boutique operation, there are 10, 20, 30, and 40 year Tawnies, and the Vintage.

Warre

📍 *Travessa do Barão de Forrester, 86, 4400 Vila Nova de Gaia*

📞 *(351) 223 776 300*

@ *warre@warre.com*

🌐 *http://www.warre.com*

🍾 *LBV, 2010*

🚫 ✖ G N

27 ha; 8,800,000 bottles, 100% Port

An old Port shipper, in fact the oldest of the British Houses, dating from 1670, Warre's started as a trading company, and took its present name in the eighteenth century when the Warre family became the dominant partners. Their control lasted until the late nineteenth century, and the first Symington became involved at the start of the twentieth century. The firm was jointly owned by Symingtons and Warres until the Symingtons took complete control in the 1960s. The Ports used to be considered to be on the lighter side, but gained force in the 1980s. Since Symingtons bought Quinta da Cavadinha (near Pinhão) in 1980, its grapes have been at the heart of Warre's Vintage Port (previously Cavadinha contributed to Fonseca). It often makes a single vineyard Port in undeclared vintages. The other major source is Quinta do Retiro Antigo, to the south of Pinhão in the Rio Torto valley, which has provided grapes for Warre's since 1935, and which the Symingtons purchased in 2006. Warre's best known Port may be Warre's Warrior, a Ruby Reserve, that's been made since the 1750s. Warre's style lies between the elegance of Graham and the solidity of Dow, its partners in the Symington stable. It's known for its LBV—"Warre's LBV is unusually fine," said Rupert Symington when I said I had confused it with Vintage in a blind tasting. It spends four years in cask and then a further four years in bottle before release. The Vintage Ports are not as rich as Graham or Dow, but are known for their aromatic qualities.

Index of Estates

INTELLIGENT GUIDES TO WINES & TOP VINEYARDS

WINES OF FRANCE SERIES

1 Bordeaux

2 Southwest France

3 Burgundy: Chablis & Côte d'Or

4 Southern Burgundy, Beaujolais & Jura

5 Champagne

6 Alsace

7 The Loire

8 The Rhône

9 Languedoc

10 Provence and Corsica

WINE OF EUROPE SERIES

11 Barolo & Barbaresco

12 Tuscany (coming soon)

13 Port & the Douro

NEW WORLD WINE SERIES

14 Napa Valley & Sonoma

BOOKS by Benjamin Lewin MW

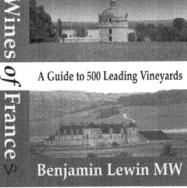

Wines of France

This comprehensive account of the vineyards and wines of France today is extensively illustrated with photographs and maps of each wine-producing area. Leading vineyards and winemakers are profiled in detail, with suggestions for wines to try and vineyards to visit.

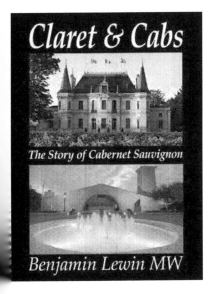

Claret & Cabs:
the Story of Cabernet Sauvignon

This worldwide survey of Cabernet Sauvignon and its blends extends from Bordeaux through the New World, defines the character of the wine from each region, and profiles leading producers.

In Search of Pinot Noir

Pinot Noir is a uniquely challenging grape with an unrivalled ability to reflect the character of the site where it grows. This world wide survey of everywhere Pinot Noir is grown extends from Burgundy to the New World, and profiles leading producers.

Wine Myths and Reality

Extensively illustrated with photographs, maps, and charts, this behind-the-scenes view of winemaking reveals the truth about what goes into a bottle of wine. Its approachable and entertaining style immediately engages the reader in the wine universe.

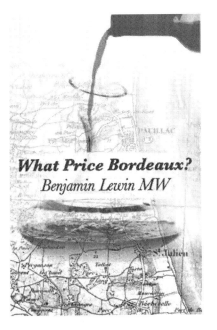

What Price Bordeaux?

A revolution is underway in Bordeaux. Top chateaux have been obtaining unprecedented prices for their wines, while smaller chateaux are going bankrupt. Extending from the changing character of Bordeaux wines to market forces, this unique overview reveals the forces making Bordeaux wine what it is today.

About the Author

Benjamin Lewin MW brings a unique combination of qualifications in wine and science to bear on the world of wine. He is one of only 300 Masters of Wine, and was the founding Editor of *Cell* journal. His previous books received worldwide critical acclaim for their innovative approach. Lewin also writes the myths and realities column in the *World of Fine Wine*, and contributes to *Decanter* magazine, *Wine & Spirits*, among others. His blog on wine is at *www.lewinonwine.com*. He divides his time between the eastern United States and the wine-growing regions of Europe, and is presently working on his next book.

Made in the USA
Lexington, KY
23 January 2017